Copyright © 2013 by Child of this Culture L.L.C.

All rights reserved. No part of this publication may be reproduced, distributed, or transmitted in any form or by any means, including photocopying, recording, or other elecronic or mechanical methods, without the prior written permission of the publisher, except in the case of brief quotations embodied in critical reviews and certain other noncommercial uses permitted by copyright law. For permission requests, write to the publisher, addressed "Attention: Permissions Coordinator" at the address below.

Child of this Culture L.L.C.
3121 Pell Mell Drive
Orlando, Florida 32818
www.childofthisculture.om

Ordering Information:
Quantity sales. Special discounts are available on quantity purchases by corporations, associations, and others.

For details, contact the publisher at the address above.

FOR OUR BROTHER ROBERTITO

THIS BOOK BELONGS TO:

I AM HIP HOP

By Cindy & Patrick Foley
Illustrations By Nathaniel Rios
Concept By Candy Molia
Layout & Lettering by Cushy Gigs

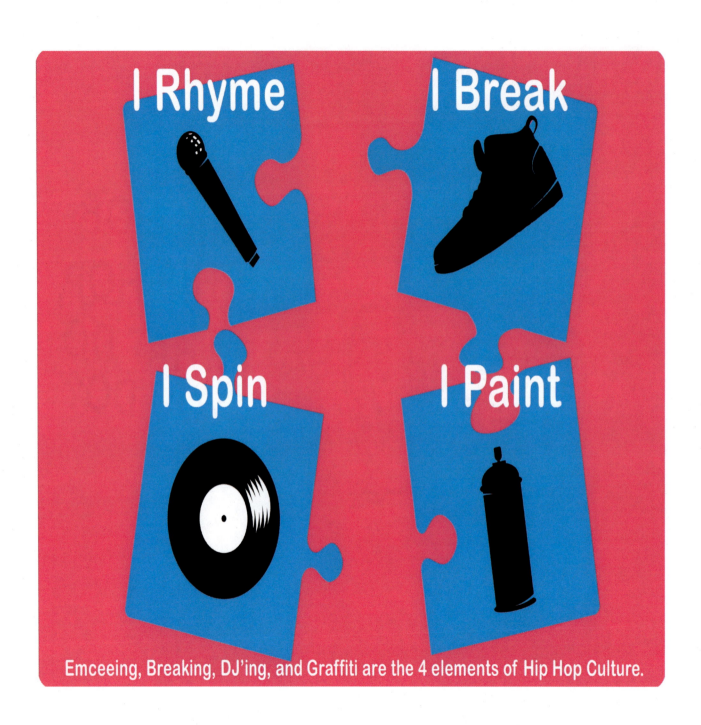

I Am Hip Hop, That's What I Do.

Hip Hop was born in the Bronx, a borough in New York City.

I Spin Records Full of Music, For One and All.

We Dance To The Break of the Beat.

We Are Hip Hop, That's What We Do.

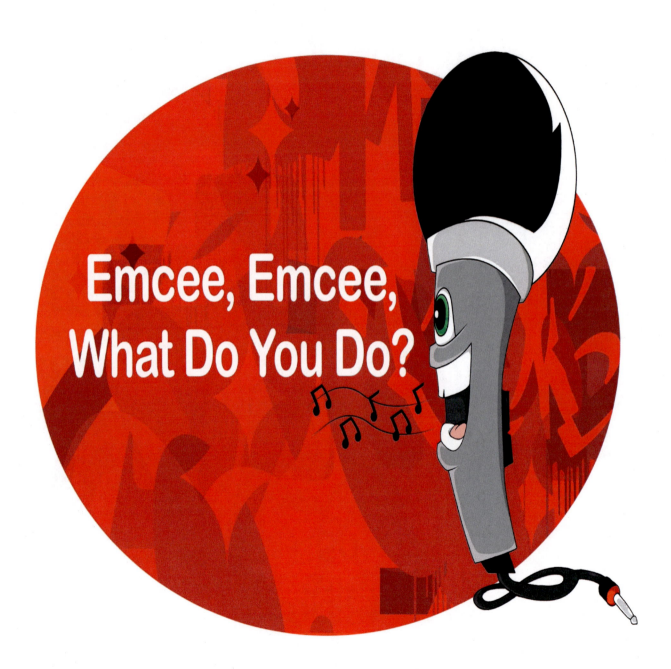

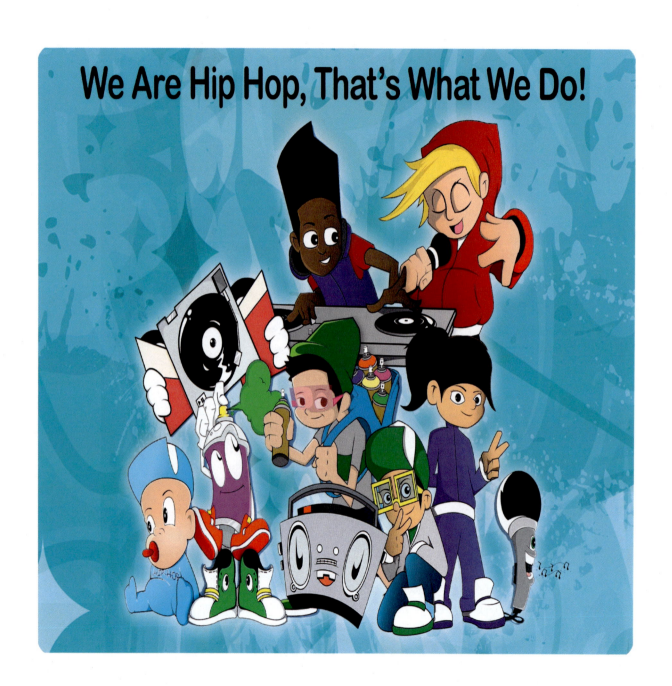

Child of this Culture was established as an organization in 2012 by twin sisters, Candy Molia and Cindy Foley. As founders of the first all female breaking group called Floor Angelz Crew; they broke gender boundaries in the late 1990's and 2000's by competing, judging, and promoting events in Orlando, Florida.

"As mothers, we wanted to improve the image of Hip Hop culture to the public, specifically the youth." states Cindy Foley. "So, we developed a book to educate and promote literacy for kids as young as 2 years old," says Candy Molia.

Child of this Culture now extends its Hip Hop arts education programs to communities across the United States, Puerto Rico, and now the rest of the world with its release of the "I am Hip Hop" book series.

For more information about Child of this Culture, visit us at www.childofthisculture.com

Made in the USA
Columbia, SC
17 June 2023

17919508R00015